AF585101

Australian States *and Territories*

TASMANIA

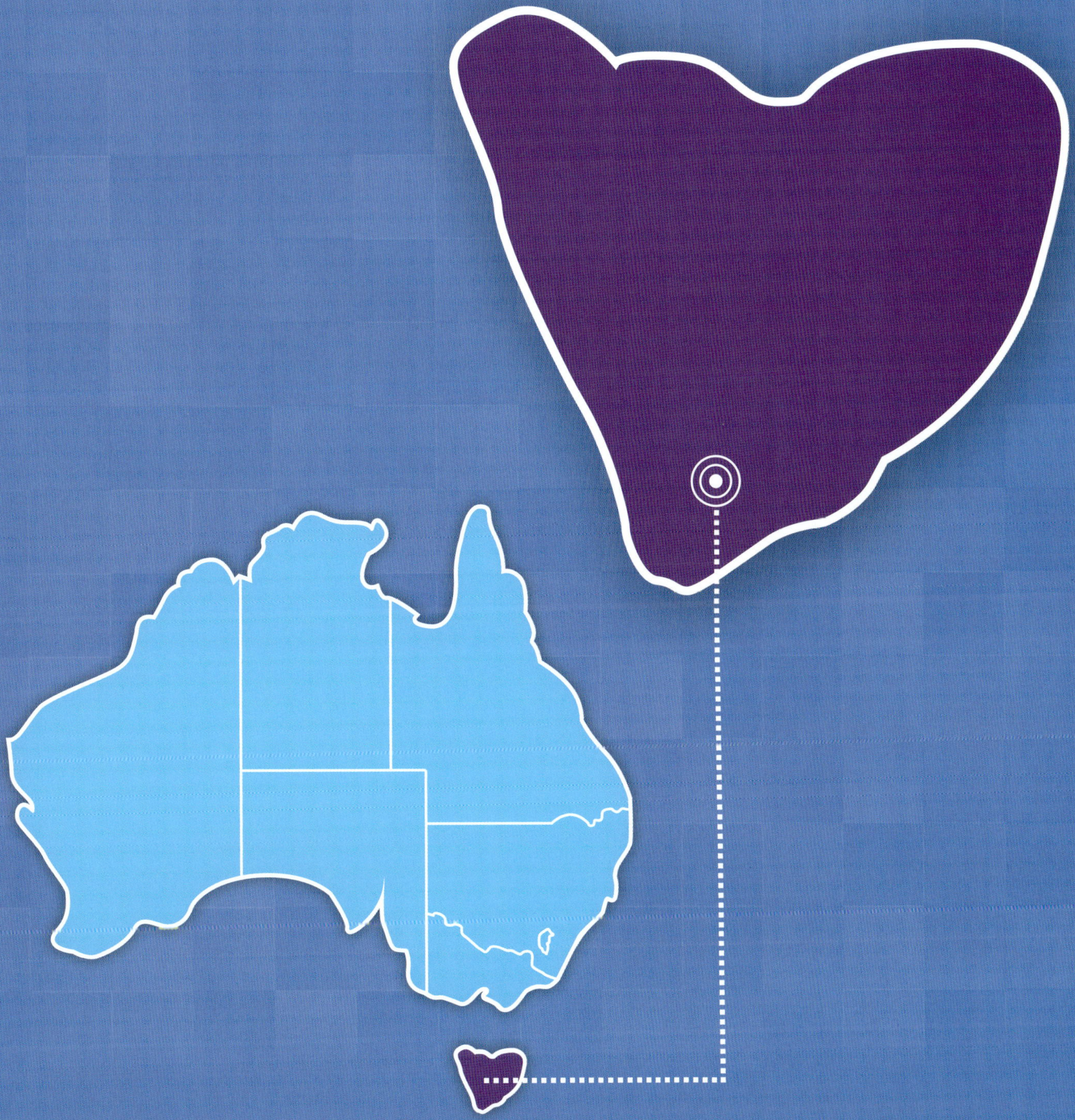

Linsie Tan

Redback Publishing
PO Box 357 Frenchs Forest NSW 2086
Australia

ISBN 978-0-9946247-5-8

First published 2017
Reprinted 2018

Author: Linsie Tan
Editor: Jane Hinchey
Original illustrations © Redback Publishing 2017
Originated by Redback Publishing
Printed and bound in China by Leo Paper

Acknowledgements
We would like to thank the following for permission to reproduce photographs: Tasmanian Archive and Heritage Office, Sgt. David J. Hercher, Nathaniel Dance-Holland, Tannatt David, Trainiac, Hothguard11, Diego Delso, ElPhantomero, jeffowenphotos, Jorge Láscar, Australian Greens Senators, Bild Bundesarchiv, yeti hunter, bilby, Peripitus, Dpulitzer, Nobel Foundation, Kr.afol, Squiresy92.

Every effort has been made to contact copyright holders of any material reproduced in this book. Any omissions will be rectified in subsequent printings if notice is given to the publisher.

Cataloguing-in-Publication details are available from the National Library of Australia

CONTENTS

Some words are shown in red, **like this**. You can find out what they mean by looking in the glossary.

Geography of Tasmania

The state of Tasmania is an island south of the mainland of Australia, across Bass Strait. Hobart on the Derwent River is the capital city.

Tasmania was linked to the rest of Australia by dry land during the last Ice Age, about 12,000 years ago. When this Ice Age ended, rising sea levels isolated Tasmania. The plants and animals already there continued to evolve in isolation from the rest of the world.

The Regions of Tasmania

Tasmania has many beautiful natural features, and its wilderness areas are some of the most pristine to be found anywhere.

Bass Strait Islands

Tasmania has two large island groups in Bass Strait. The biggest islands in these groups are King Island and Flinders Island.

King Island

Known for its exceptional dairy produce, King Island is 80 kilometres from Tasmania. The strong winds and rocky coastline have resulted in many tragic shipwrecks.

Flinders Island

This is the largest of the Furneaux Island Group. Flinders Island was used as a place of exile for Aboriginal people from 1833. It is now a tourist destination, offering visitors a mild climate, beaches, mountains and historic sites to explore.

Alpine Regions

The alpine highlands are in the west of Tasmania, and also in the Ben Lomond National Park in the northeast. Alpine regions include both treeless moorland as well as pine forests.

West Coast

Tasmania's west coast towns provide tourist access to the Franklin and Gordon Rivers and the World Heritage wilderness areas. Other features of the west coast are Macquarie Harbour, the Sarah Island convict buildings and Queenstown, an historic copper mining site.

Southern Region and Hobart

Hobart, the capital of Tasmania, is a port city. Further inland, the Derwent Valley is a rural area that contributes fruits, potatoes, hops and wine to Tasmania's agricultural output. Farmers in the Huon Valley area grow apples, and Tasmania's salmon fishing industry operates from the south coast.

Northern Region and Launceston

Launceston, the second largest city in Tasmania, is on the Tamar River. Agricultural produce of the northern region includes fruits, lavender and grapes. The homesteads of Woolmers and Brickendon are World Heritage listed and reveal the village lifestyle of colonial settlers living on large estates.

Highlands

The highland plateau in the central region of Tasmania is a diverse region, with both mountains and pastures. There are many mountain lakes on the high plateau, one of which is Lake St Clair, the deepest lake in Australia and the source of the Derwent River.

Population

The population of Tasmania is about 518,000 people (2016)

Climate

Tasmania's climate is mild to cold. Although rainfall is usually regular, farmers occasionally suffer the effects of drought.

PREDICT THE POPULATION

Draw a graph and use it to estimate what the population will be in 2050.

YEAR	1850	1900	1950	2000	2050
POPULATION	69,000	173,000	290,000	473,000	?

FAST FACTS

- **Highest recorded temperature: Scamander, 42.2°C in 2009**
- **Lowest recorded temperature: Tarraleah Village, - 13°C in 1983**

WORD FILE

pristine - clean and unspoiled
plateau - a flat and high area of the landscape

Tasmanian Fact File

Highest mountain in Tasmania - Mount Ossa, 1,617 metres high
Longest river in Tasmania - the South Esk River, 252 kilometres long
Oldest public building in Tasmania - the Commissariat Store built between 1808 and 1810
Australia's oldest stone arch bridge - Richmond Bridge over the Coal River, built in 1825
Most southerly point of Australia - South East Cape

Aboriginal History of Tasmania

Aboriginal people have lived in Tasmania for about 35,000 years. They developed complex societies and ways of life, and their culture depends on having a strong spiritual relationship with the land.

There are many different Aboriginal nations, each with its own lands and cultural traditions. A nation is defined by its connection to its land and by its language. Groups within a nation may also have their own dialects.

Some of the Tasmanian Aboriginal nation or language groups at the time of colonisation:

- Lairmairrener
- Nuenonne
- Paredarerme
- Peerapper
- Pyemmairre
- Tommeginne
- Toogee
- Tyerremotepanner

European Settlers and the Aboriginal Nations

The Aboriginal nations had strong relationships with the land, and this caused conflict between them and the European settlers. Cattle and sheep replaced native food animals on the land, and settlers colonised areas that had been in traditional ownership for thousands of years.

Aboriginal History Timeline for Tasmania

35,000 years ago — Ancestors of the Aboriginal people migrated into Tasmania when it was joined to the rest of Australia by dry land.

10,000 years ago — Rising sea levels turned Tasmania into an island and isolated its people.

Before colonisation — The Aboriginal population of Tasmania was possibly up to 10,000 people.

1820s — Intense conflict between Aboriginal people and settlers became known as the Black War.

1830 — The Black Line was a violent campaign by colonists to drive all Aboriginal people off the land and to force them into one location.

1833 — Aboriginal people were sent to Flinders Island. The settlement there was called Wybalenna.

Wybalenna

Ancient History of Tasmania

To find out what life was like in the ancient past of Tasmania, archaeologists may look for:

- stone structures built in waterways to trap fish
- stone quarries
- canoe trees
- shell middens
- remains of dome huts

Australian Aboriginal Artefacts

Aboriginal Archaeological Sites in Tasmania

Toolumbunner in the Gog Range - This is the site of a large ochre quarry used by Aboriginal people as a source of ingredients to make paint for ceremonial body art and rock wall painting.

Rock Art Sites - In the Preminghana Indigenous Protected Area, in the northwest, and at Greens Creek in the west of Tasmania.

Truganini 1812 - 1876

Truganini is the most well-known Aboriginal person in Tasmanian history. Although she is often called the last surviving Aboriginal person in the state, this is not correct, and many other Tasmanian Aboriginal people have descendants living today.

Truganini (seated, right)

Truganini's life was one of sadness and courage. European settlers, including farmers and whalers, killed many of her close family. Despite this she was pragmatic and did her best to preserve the lives of those still remaining. The Aboriginal people were removed to a settlement on Flinders Island and Truganini realised that, although this was not ideal, anyone not on the settlement was likely to be killed by the colonists. After her death in Hobart, her skeleton was put on display in the Tasmanian Museum, an act which was in direct conflict with her final wishes. It was not until 1976 that Truganini's remains received a traditional burial.

Fire and the Landscape

Aboriginal people altered their land using fire to produce more open grassed areas. This made hunting easier. Some of the grassy plains now used as pastures by farmers may have been developed over thousands of years through Aboriginal fire management.

Crafts

Craft in the form of intricate basket weaving and the creation of jewellery from shells was highly developed in Tasmanian Aboriginal society and continues to be an artistic pursuit today.

Food Sources

Food was plentiful and included meat from land animals, fish and shellfish, eggs and a vast variety of plants and fruits.

Trade

Trade between different nations occurred throughout Tasmania. This included the trade of objects and raw materials, and probably also the exchange of cultural ideas.

WORD FILE

dialects - different forms of the one language
colonise - to settle in a new land and impose a new culture on the people living there
traditional ownership - the Aboriginal land ownership system in existence before the arrival of Europeans

Colonial History of Tasmania

European and Colonial History Timeline

1642 Abel Tasman, a Dutch explorer, reached the west coast of Tasmania. He named it Van Diemen's Land after the Governor of the Dutch East Indies.

1777 James Cook anchored his ship in the bay near Bruny Island.

1792 A French explorer discovered a large river on the southeast coast.

1793 John Hayes renamed the river discovered by the French, calling it the Derwent River.

1798 Bass and Flinders circumnavigated Tasmania, proving that it was an island and not part of the mainland.

1803 Governor King, the Governor of New South Wales and Van Diemen's Land, sent Lieutenant John Bowen to establish a convict settlement on the banks of the Derwent River. The aim was to discourage the French from claiming the island.

1804 David Collins was appointed Lieutenant Governor of Van Diemen's Land. He established the settlement that became Hobart. Van Diemen's Land was used as a place of punishment for the worst convicts from New South Wales.

1804 Lieutenant Colonel Paterson founded a settlement on the Tamar River, close to the site which later became Launceston.

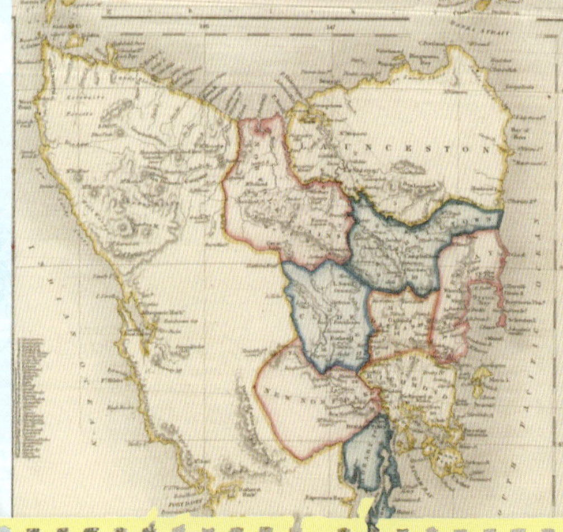

1812 The first ship carrying convicts directly from England arrived.

1825 Van Diemen's Land became a separate colony.

1853 The last convict ship arrived in Hobart.

1856 The colony was renamed Tasmania.

WORD FILE

circumnavigate - to sail all around a land mass

Antarctic Exploration

Hobart became a point of departure for the great Antarctic explorers during the early 20th century. They included Roald Amundsen, who led the first expedition to reach the South Pole. After achieving this feat in 1911, Amundsen and his team returned to Hobart to spread the news. Another explorer who left from Hobart was Douglas Mawson. His Antarctic expedition of 1911 to 1914 mapped the coastline and performed scientific investigations.

Dr. Mackay, Professor David, Douglas Mawson

FAST FACTS

- **After the discovery of Bass Strait in 1798, ships began using it instead of having to sail all the way around Tasmania. This made the journey much faster.**
- **Coal River was named in 1803 by a small group of explorers, led by Lieutenant John Bowen, after the discovery of coal in the river.**
- **The Mercury newspaper first appeared in 1854 and is still being published today.**

Transport in Tasmania

Pre-Colonial Transport

The first methods of transport used by Aboriginal people in Australia were walking and paddling canoes. Canoes were made of bark or from hollowed out logs, and they were used for fishing and to cross rivers and harbours. 'Canoe trees' are important reminders of this early technology.

Road Transport

Convicts provided the labour to build the first roads in the colony. Settlers either walked, rode horses, or used horses and bullocks to pull carts along the bumpy, uneven surfaces.

The first horse-drawn coach service began in Tasmania in 1829. Coach services were expensive and the poor roads made them very uncomfortable.

Railways and Buses

Tasmania stopped running passenger trains in 1978. TasRail now only operates freight services, which link key towns to each other and to ports. Buses have become the main form of public transport.

Historic railways still operate in a number of locations around Tasmania. These railways were once the only way remote towns could deliver their mining and agricultural products to markets and ports.

Sailing Ships

Sailing ships were important for Tasmania's early development, both for travel to the mainland, and to provide transport around the coast between local ports.

The sea around Tasmania hides many shipwrecks, victims of the rocky coastlines and the Roaring Forties, a strong westerly wind. One of these ships, the Sydney Cove, was wrecked in Bass Street in 1797. Its remains were only discovered in 1977.

Air Transport

The first commercial airline in Tasmania began flights in 1931. It flew between Hobart, Launceston and Melbourne. There are now five main airports in Tasmania, a comparatively large number considering the small population of the state.

Trams

The first tram began operating in Hobart in 1893. Trams ceased running in 1960, when buses and motor cars became a more popular means of transport. Hobart was unique in having the only double-decker trams in Australia. A restored example of one of these is in the Tasmanian Transport Museum. Launceston also had its own tram service, which provided public transport around the city from 1911 to 1952.

Ports

Since Tasmania is an island, sea ports are very important for linking the state to the rest of Australia. There are four large shipping ports in Tasmania:

- Bell Bay Port
- Burnie Port
- Devonport Port
- Hobart Port

They provide infrastructure for handling bulk goods from mining operations and forestry. The Shiploader at the Burnie Port is vital for Tasmania's minerals exporting industry.

There are also regional ports used by fishing and tourism vessels.

Ferry

Spirit of Tasmania is a large ferry that carries passengers and vehicles across the Bass Strait from Melbourne in Victoria to Devonport in Tasmania. The voyage takes about ten hours and passengers can take their cars on board.

WHAT DO YOU THINK?

Why are there so many airports in Tasmania?
Why did the tram services all cease operating?

WORD FILE

infrastructure - buildings and physical services needed by a community

Tasmania, the Wilderness State

Tasmanian Wilderness World Heritage Area

The Tasmanian Wilderness World Heritage Area covers 1.58 million hectares, which is about a quarter of the state. The wilderness protects some flora and fauna that are now extinct on the mainland of Australia. The area also contains significant Aboriginal sites.

Plants and Animals of the World Heritage Area

The protected wilderness of Tasmania has a range of environments, including moorlands, ancient pine forests, temperate rainforests, coastal and alpine areas. Some of the plants are descendants of species that have been growing there for millions of years, since the time when Tasmania was a part of the ancient continent of Gondwana.

There are extensive cave systems included in the heritage area. The Marakoopa Cave, which is open to the public, contains deposits from the last ice-age, as well as fascinating cave fauna, such as glow worms and the Tasmanian cave spider.

The majority of the animal species of Tasmania live within the World Heritage Area. Some of these animals include the moss froglet, eastern quoll and Tasmanian pademelon.

Cultural Heritage

The World Heritage Site was selected for both its natural features and its cultural importance. One of the sites that archaeologists have investigated is the Kutikina Cave. The rock art, tools and remains of human habitation found there show that Aboriginal people were living in the cave up to 30,000 years ago. This included periods during the last Ice Age when the climate was much colder than today. The Aboriginal people in Tasmania at that time were possibly the only people living so far south in the whole world.

Where is the World Heritage Area in Tasmania?

The World Heritage Area is managed by the Parks and Wildlife Service of Tasmania. There are a number of national parks and reserves that make up the wilderness region:

- Central Plateau Conservation Area
- Cradle Mountain
- Devils Gullet State Reserve
- Hartz Mountains
- Lake St Clair
- Liffey Falls State Reserve
- Mole Creek Karst National Park
- Southwest National Park
- Walls of Jerusalem National Park
- Wild Rivers National Park

FAST FACT

In the 1980s, the proposed damming of the Franklin and Gordon Rivers was opposed by people who were concerned that this would damage the wilderness.

Threats to the World Heritage Area

The Parks and Wildlife Service has identified the following threats to the World Heritage Area, and has produced action plans to deal with them:

- Drought and climate change
- Fire
- Illegal activities such as logging or hunting
- Devil facial tumour disease in Tasmanian devils
- Plant diseases
- Weeds
- Pest animals
- Impacts from tourism
- Building of new structures
- Erosion along the coast
- Preservation of Aboriginal heritage
- Hydroelectric power developments

Industries and Business in Tasmania

Tourism

Tourism is an important source of income for Tasmania. People visit the state to experience wilderness areas, exceptional farm produce and historic tourist sites. The preserved Georgian and Victorian buildings throughout the state make Tasmania a favoured destination for people interested in colonial history.

Whaling

Whaling was one of Tasmania's first industries, and both local and foreign whaling ships used ports around Tasmania's coast. Oil was extracted from the whale carcasses at whaling stations, and sold internationally for use in lighting and on machinery. Whale bones were used to make women's corsets. The Tasmanian whaling industry ended around 1900.

Mining and Minerals

Mining and mineral processing combined provide about 50 per cent of Tasmania's export income. Minerals extracted include copper, iron, gold, lead, silver, tin, zinc and silica. Coal from Tasmania was exported by ship to the early colony in New South Wales, where it was used for heating and cooking. Coal is still mined in Tasmania.

Oil and Gas

The search for petroleum under the sea around Tasmania began in the1960s. Offshore drilling for natural gas operates from marine platforms in Bass Strait, and the product is processed in Victoria. The Tasmanian Natural Gas Pipeline carries gas from Victoria to Tasmania under the waters of Bass Strait.

Shipbuilding

Shipbuilding and repair services in Tasmania represent about 5 per cent of the total shipbuilding industry in Australia. Shipbuilding has been a local industry since colonial times.

Commercial Fishing

Tasmania has a thriving fishing industry. Fishing for rock lobsters has been a mainstay of the industry for over 150 years, while the farming of Atlantic salmon in Tasmania began in the 1980s. Tasmania produces 25 per cent of the world's wild abalone.

Antarctic Services

Hobart is one of the few cities in the world which provides facilities for ships and aircraft leaving for the Antarctic, whether for scientific research or for tourism.

The Tasmanian Polar Network has been formed to provide a network of business and professional services for activities which focus on the Antarctic and the Southern Ocean.

Forestry

The forest industry maintains a balance between the protection of native forests and ensuring that the logging of trees continues to provide income and employment for Tasmanians. Broad scale clearing of native forests no longer occurs and the Tasmanian government encourages forestry businesses to make use of the total logging product, rather than leaving any as waste.

Agriculture in Tasmania

One quarter of the land in Tasmania is used for agriculture, and this small state accounts for a large proportion of Australia's vegetable production and export.

Vegetables, Grains and Fruit

Apples, Stone Fruit, Berries - Tasmania has a long history of apple growing.
Peas and Beans - Most of the peas and beans consumed in Australia are grown in Tasmania.
Grains - Crops include barley, wheat and oats.
Potatoes - Tasmania produces one of the largest crops of potatoes in Australia.
Onions - Most of Australia's exported onions are grown in Tasmania.

Dairying

Tasmania's reliable rainfall and rich pastures produce high quality dairy products. Specialty cheeses from dairies located in Tasmania and the Bass Strait islands have a reputation that makes them sought after by consumers worldwide.

Meats

The ban on genetically modified products, and on added hormones in livestock, contributes to Tasmania's reputation as a source of natural and safe foods. Local meats include beef, lamb and venison.

Merino Wool

Tasmanian sheep farmers produce superfine wool from Merino sheep. More than 95 per cent of this wool is exported to Japan, China, Germany and Italy.

Opiates

Tasmania is a legal supplier of opiates for the pharmaceutical industry. It produces about 45 per cent of the world's opiates from poppies.

Pyrethrum

Tasmania produces about 60 per cent of the world's pyrethrum from plants. Pyrethrum is an insecticide.

Lavender and Other Plant Oils

The therapeutic and cosmetic industries around the world source many of their essential oils from farms in Tasmania. Products include the oils from lavender, peppermint and many other plants.

Flowers and Garden Products

Tasmanian growers produce cut flowers, bulbs, seeds and fertilisers.

MENU
RESTAURANT

WORK IT OUT

Design a meal menu that uses only foods grown in Tasmania.

WORD FILE

opiates - drugs derived from the opium poppy

Environment and Sustainability in Tasmania

Sustainable practices for agriculture and industry require a balance between using the land and waterways for development and keeping areas as regions of natural beauty.

Bushfires

Tasmania's delicate alpine regions, its rainforests and its World Heritage Area are all susceptible to severe damage if a bushfire occurs. Regeneration in these areas can be very slow, sometimes taking many years. The Huon Pine, for example, may not reach its full height until it is 1,000 years old.

RESOURCES	HOW WE CAN LOOK AFTER THEM
SOIL	Correct use of fertilisers and avoiding soil erosion
WATER	Keeping water supplies unpolluted
NATIVE PLANTS	Avoid complete clearing of areas for pastures
NATIVE ANIMALS	Keep some areas of natural bushland for food and shelter
AIR QUALITY	Avoid polluting the air through poor industrial practices

Some plants and animals in Tasmania have evolved to take advantage of bushfires:

- Banksia seedpods need the heat of a fire to open.
- The New Holland mouse population increases after a bushfire as there are more seeds for them to eat.
- Since the Tasmanian bettong finds food in open grassland, its population can increase if bushes and undergrowth are burnt away.

Black Tuesday bushfires in 1967 were one of Australia's worst natural disasters. As well as destroying forests they also damaged farms, towns and parts of Hobart.

The Tasmania Fire Service employs highly trained firefighters and also relies on thousands of volunteers throughout the state.

Protecting Native Plants and Animals

Many species of plants and animals are under threat in Tasmania. Threats include introduced species and the destruction of natural habitats.

Tasmanian Tiger

In 1936, the last known thylacine, or Tasmanian tiger, died in a zoo in Hobart. This animal was a dog-sized marsupial carnivore and farmers hunted it to stop the attacks on their livestock. Although there are occasional reports of the Tasmanian tiger being seen in remote bushland, it is probably extinct.

Tasmanian Devil

The Tasmanian Devil is a small, marsupial carnivore. It became extinct on the mainland about 400 years ago and Tasmania is its last stronghold. The Tasmanian Devil's continued existence is threatened by Devil Facial Tumour Disease. Healthy populations have been released into controlled areas to try to stop the spread of the disease and ensure that the Tasmanian Devil does not become extinct.

FAST FACTS

Pest animals already in Tasmania include:

- **Feral cats, dogs and goats**
- **Rabbits**
- **Feral pigs on Flinders Island**

Renewable Energy

Renewable sources of energy can come from water, wind and solar power. Although Tasmania draws some power via the Basslink undersea cable from the Australian mainland, the state is proud of the fact that it can generate a proportion of its electricity from renewable sources. The Tamar Valley power station uses gas as a fuel but most of the locally generated electricity in Tasmania comes from hydro-power.

Wind Farms

Tasmania runs wind farms at Studland Bay, Bluff Point, Musselroe and King Island. The extreme winds known as the Roaring Forties were once the cause of many shipwrecks off the Tasmanian coast, but they are now a wind resource for Tasmania.

Food Production

Tasmania differentiates itself from other larger producers of food by stressing that its products are 'clean and green'.

- Livestock is largely disease-free.
- There is a ban on added hormones.
- There are high animal welfare standards.
- The planting of genetically modified crops is banned.

THINK TANK

Dogs and other pets are not allowed in national parks in Tasmania. What do you think is the reason for this restriction?

Biosecurity

The native plants and animals that exist in Tasmania have developed over years of isolation. To preserve the unique features of its natural environment, and to stop the spread of imported diseases and pests, Tasmania regulates all live animal imports:

- The import of foxes, dingoes, pigeons, rainbow lorikeets and queen bees is banned.
- Pet dogs can only be imported if they meet strict health requirements.
- Keeping freshwater turtles as pets is not allowed.

Water Supply

Although Tasmania has an extensive system of rivers and water catchments, drought can still affect the water supply for farming and domestic use. Taswater runs education programs that stress the need for conserving water, keeping catchment areas clean, and taking care not to wash pollutants into any waterway.

WORD FILE

biosecurity - controlling plants, insects and animals that are harmful

Government of Tasmania

Timeline for Government in Tasmania

Before colonisation
Tasmanian Aboriginal nations governed according to their own laws.

Until 1825 Van Diemen's Land was administered from Sydney.

1825 Van Diemen's Land became a separate colony.

1856 The colony was renamed Tasmania and its bicameral government met for the first time.

1901 Federation meant that Tasmania became a state of Australia.

1904 Women were allowed to vote in Tasmania.

1922 Women were allowed to stand for election to parliament in Tasmania.

FAST FACTS
'Terra nullius' is Latin for 'land that nobody owns'. The British government used this idea to allow them to claim the island of Van Diemen's Land.

Premiers of Tasmania

The first Premier of Tasmania was William Champ in 1856. The first female Premier was Lara Giddings in 2011.

Government House

Government House was built in 1857 and was designed by William Porden Kay. It is an example of a Victorian era country house and is one of the largest of its style in Australia. The building replaced the first Government House, which was constructed in Macquarie Street, Hobart, in 1817.

Government House 1878

Parliament House 1878

Parliament House

The building that houses Tasmania's parliament was built in 1840 and initially used as a Customs House. The early Legislative Council met there in 1841 and the building was later altered to accommodate the first colonial parliament in 1856.

Local Government

There are 29 local government councils in Tasmania. Some of the services they are responsible for are:

- Local roads
- Rubbish collection
- Parks and ovals
- Public swimming pools
- Community halls

FAST FACT

There are only 5 electorates in Tasmania: Bass, Braddon, Denison, Franklin, Lyons

The Tasmanian Parliament Today

Tasmania has a bicameral state government.

The Legislative Council (Upper House) has 15 members
The House of Assembly (Lower House) has 25 members

The Hansard is a record of what the politicians say in parliament. To find out more about what the elected members have said about your own school or suburb in the Tasmanian parliament, search the Hansard at www.parliament.tas.gov.au/ParliamentSearch/

WORD FILE

bicameral - a government having two houses or sections

Notable People from Tasmania

Elizabeth Blackburn (1948 -)
Elizabeth Blackburn was born in Hobart. She is a molecular biologist and was awarded a Nobel Prize for her research into genes and telomeres. Her work has implications for ageing and cancer treatments. She was the first Australian woman to receive a Nobel Prize.

Errol Flynn (1909 - 1959)
Errol Flynn was a Tasmanian actor who became a Hollywood star and celebrity during the mid 1900s. In his many films, his characters were usually daring adventurers.

Enid Lyons (1897 - 1981)
Enid Lyons was the first woman elected to the Australian House of Representatives. She was born in Tasmania, which is where she trained as a teacher. Her husband was Joseph Lyons, the Prime Minister in 1931, and after his death she decided to run for election herself. Her legacy is the introduction of welfare payments for mothers, and promoting equality for women in the workplace.

Ricky Ponting (1974 -)
Ricky Ponting was born in Launceston. He was captain of the Australian cricket team from 2004 to 2011. Named Cricketer of the Decade 2000, he is one of the best batsmen of his time.

Mary Donaldson (1972 -)
After her marriage in 2004 to Crown Prince Frederik, heir to the Danish throne, Mary Donaldson became Crown Princess Mary of Denmark. Born in Hobart, Mary Donaldson studied law and commerce, and worked in advertising and real estate before meeting Prince Frederik.

Harold Gatty (1903 - 1957)
Harold Gatty was a Tasmanian inventor and aviator. His ground-speed and drift indicator revolutionised navigation for pilots and formed the basis of later developments which led to the auto-pilot system. In 1951, he founded Fiji's first airline service. There is a memorial park named after him in Campbell Town.

Peter Sculthorpe (1929 - 2014)
An Australian music composer, Peter Sculthorpe was born in Launceston. His work was influenced by Australian culture, Australian Indigenous music and by Indonesian music. In 1997, he was named as one of Australia's 100 Living National Treasures, and in 2001 he was awarded an Order of Australia.

Lucy Beeton (1829 - 1886)
Lucy Beeton was the daughter of colonial settler, Thomas Beeton, and Tasmanian Aboriginal woman, Bet Smith. Her parents ensured she received a good education and she became a successful business operator. Nicknamed Queen of the Isles, Lucy Beeton owned a fleet of boats which traded between Tasmania and the mainland.

Christopher Koch (1932 - 2013)
Born in Hobart, Christopher Koch was a renowned fiction novelist. He won the Miles Franklin Award for fiction twice, and received the Order of Australia in 1995. His novel, The Year of Living Dangerously, was made into a film in 1992 starring Mel Gibson.

Bob Brown (1944 -)
Although born in NSW, Bob Brown is known for his association with Tasmania, through his work to protect the state's environment, and as the leader of the Australian Greens from 2005 - 2012. After retiring from politics, he founded the Bob Brown Foundation, to keep the public aware of threats to the wilderness areas in Tasmania.

Immigration to Tasmania

Immigration Timeline for Tasmania

35,000 years ago Ancestors of the Aboriginal people migrated into Tasmania when it was joined to the rest of Australia by dry land.

1837 Families sailing from Ireland to Hobart in 1837 were struck with tragedy, when nearly half the 133 children on board died from illness.

1853 The last convict ship arrived in Hobart. The lack of convicts as labourers badly affected Tasmania's economy for many years. This situation was worsened when the gold rush enticed even more men to leave the state.

1930s The numbers of people migrating to Tasmania decreased during the Great Depression years as there was not enough employment to attract workers to settle there.

1940s Tasmania welcomed refugees leaving the war ravaged countries of Europe. They provided much-needed labour for building and public works.

E-Migration or a Flight of Fair Game, Alfred Ducote, 1832

FAST FACTS

In the 1800s, migration posters used in Europe claimed that Tasmania had no droughts and the best climate in the world.

Where Did They Come From?

Britain
In the 1800s, free travel was offered to tradesmen, labourers or domestic servants from Britain. These immigration schemes were very specific about the migrants they would allow to travel for free. Because of the labour shortage in the colony, they favoured men and women who were young, healthy and ready to work.

Germany
Germans were encouraged to migrate to Tasmania during the mid 1800s and up until the time of the First World War. Many of them settled near Launceston and Hobart.

China
In the late 1800s, many Chinese men arrived in Tasmania to work on the gold mines and tin fields. During this period they outnumbered the European tin miners. Nearly all the Chinese miners eventually returned to China, but a few stayed, often working as market gardeners and shopkeepers.

Poland
In 1947, after the Second World War, a small group of Polish ex-servicemen arrived in Tasmania and began working for the Hydro-Electric Commission. They had been members of the military garrison known as the Rats of Tobruk. They laboured in remote areas of Tasmania, building dams and power stations, and lived in camps in the bush.

Migrants to Tasmania have come from many countries around the world. How many of these countries can you name?

Population Growth Strategy

The Tasmanian government has created the Population Growth Strategy to boost migration through job creation and promoting the Tasmanian lifestyle. The target population for 2050 is 650,000 people. The Tasmanian government aims to achieve this using a number of migration strategies:

- International migration
- Interstate migration
- Humanitarian migration
- Retaining international students

Major Sites in Tasmania

These sites include buildings, structures and natural features. They are important for their beauty, rarity and history.

Cradle Mountain & Lake St Clair National Park

This national park in the west of the state is part of the Tasmanian Wilderness World Heritage Area. It is one of the few temperate wilderness areas in the Southern Hemisphere. The area includes Lake Pedder, which was the focus of a conservation campaign by environmentalists in the 1960s.

Port Arthur Historic Site

Port Arthur was built as a jail to house convicts and is now a tourist attraction. From 1830 to 1877 it was a place of punishment and misery. The numerous buildings and extensive grounds today present a picturesque vista for visitors and provide an insight into early colonial lifestyles.

Darlington Probation Station

A jail on Maria Island, off the east coast of Tasmania, used to house male convicts from 1842 onwards.

Cascades Female Factory

Located outside Hobart, the Cascades Female Factory housed female convicts. The accommodation included convict dormitories, solitary cells, a nursery, hospital and chapel.

The Coal Mines Historic Site

This site on the Tasman Peninsula, near Saltwater River, was the location of Tasmania's first coal mine. Convict labour was used to produce coal so that Tasmania did not have to rely on importing it from New South Wales. For over 40 years, male convicts laboured at the mine and lived in harsh conditions. Men who had been sent to Port Arthur were transferred here if they committed further crimes.

The Estates (near Longford)

The Brickendon Estate and the neighbouring Woollmers Estate have been preserved as examples of early homesteads.

Parliament House, Hobart

Parliament House in Hobart was designed by John Lee Archer, not as a home for the government, but as a Customs House. The Derwent River originally ran much closer to the building than it does today, making it easy for customs officials to inspect the cargo on ships. Sandstone for the construction was quarried at Salamanca Square, and a small railway was built to carry the heavy blocks to the building site. The Customs House was altered to accommodate the first colonial parliament in 1856, and it has been Tasmania's Parliament House ever since.

Salamanca Markets

The Salamanca Markets are one of Tasmania's tourist attractions and have been operating since 1972. In the early 1800s, the original markets for the town of Hobart were also located beside the Derwent River, not far from the modern Salamanca Markets.

World Heritage Areas in Tasmania

- Tasmanian Wilderness
- Port Arthur Historic Site
- Cascades Female Factory
- Darlington Probation Station
- Coal Mines Historic Site
- Estates (near Longford)

Wrest Point Casino

Wrest Point Casino, the first legal casino in Australia, was opened at Sandy Bay in 1973. For some years it was the only legal casino in Australia.

Macquarie Island

This island is a remote wilderness area, with a rugged and beautiful coastline. It is located between Tasmania and the Antarctic.

The Tasmanian Trail

This recreational trail is 480 kilometres long and extends from Devonport in the north to Dover in the south. The trail passes through farmland, natural areas and towns, and it gives the active visitor a chance to experience a range of Tasmania's magnificent and interesting locations.

Flags, Symbols, Emblems and Special Days of of Tasmania

People living in Tasmania use flags, symbols and special days to show their connection to their community. These connections include pride for the group they belong to, an interest in history, and wanting to join others for celebrations that bring people together.

Tasmanian State Flag

The Tasmanian state flag was officially proclaimed in 1975, but a similar design has been used since 1875. The Union Jack represents the state's historic ties with Britain.

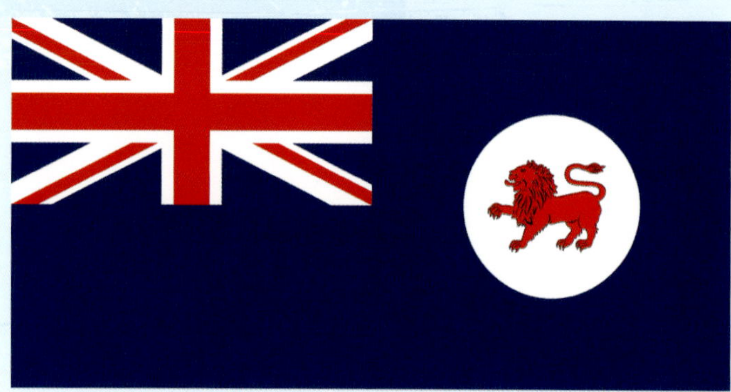

Australian Aboriginal Flag

The Aboriginal Flag was first flown in 1971. It was designed by Elder Harold Thomas.
Yellow disc - the sun and yellow ochre
Red - the land
Black - the Aboriginal people of Australia

RULES FOR FLYING THESE FLAGS

- **Don't fly more than one on the same pole.**
- **Don't fly them in the dark.**
- **Raise the flag to the top of the pole before lowering it to half-mast.**
- **Treat these flags with respect.**

The Tasmanian Coat of Arms

- Two Tasmanian tigers support a shield topped by a lion.
- The Latin motto 'Ubertas et Fidelitas' means ´Fruitfulness and Faithfulness´.
- The wheat, apples, hops and sheep on the shield represent agriculture.
- The red lion holding a pick and shovel represents mining.

Symbols of Tasmania

Floral Emblem - Tasmanian flowering blue gum
Animal Emblem - Tasmanian devil
Mineral Emblem - Crocoite

Special Days

Australia Day - On 26th January each year, Australians commemorate the founding of a British colony by Governor Phillip at Sydney Cove in 1788.

ANZAC Day - Ceremonies and marches for ANZAC Day are held all around the state on 25th April each year. The largest march in the state is in Hobart and there are ceremonies at the Cenotaph which overlooks the Derwent River.

NAIDOC Week - A week in July each year to celebrate the history, culture and achievements of Aboriginal and Torres Strait Islander peoples. Communities and government bodies organise events around the state for NAIDOC Week.

Special Days Held Only in Tasmania

Royal Hobart Regatta Day (Southern Tasmania)
Recreation Day (Northern Tasmania)
Show Day (local holidays which are held when there is an agricultural show in the area)
Devonport Cup Day
Launceston Cup Day

Make Your Own Coat of Arms

Design a Coat of Arms for your family, club or sport group

- Use symbols that everyone will know
- Your own Coat of Arms could include drawings or pictures to tell the history of the group
- Think about where to use your Coat of Arms
- Where have you seen the Tasmanian Coat of Arms used?

WORD FILE

Elder - a respected Aboriginal person who is a custodian of traditional knowledge
half-mast - flying a flag halfway up the pole as a mark of respect when a community leader dies

How to Find Out More
Primary and Secondary Sources

There are many ways to find out more about Tasmania. You can do this using both primary and secondary sources. Websites can have a mixture of both types of sources on them.

Primary Sources

- **Interviews** - when people say what they have seen
- **Letters** - when the writer was the person experiencing the event
- **Newspapers** - when the facts are presented, such as a list of prices for groceries
- **Photos** - when they have not been altered
- **Maps**
- **Old Items & Antiques**
- **News on Television** - when it shows pictures of real events
- **School Newsletters** - when they list names or dates of events
- **Videos on Youtube or Facebook** - when they show an event and have not been altered

Secondary Sources

- **Letters** - when the writer is retelling the facts that someone else told them
- **Newspapers** - when the story is told by someone who retells the facts that someone else told them
- **Photos** - when the photo has been altered
- **Songs, Poems, Stories**
- **News on Television** - when it is reported by a journalist who did not experience the events

FAST FACTS

Find old newspapers at your local library. Use these to look at pictures of areas you know and to see how they have changed over time.

Museums

Visit museums to find primary sources. You could look for examples of clothing that the convict labourers wore and compare it with the uniforms of their guards or the dresses owned by the free women settlers.

Museums in Tasmania

- The Tasmanian Museum and Art Gallery, Hobart
- MONA (Museum of Old and New Art), Berriedale
- West Coast Pioneers Memorial Museum, Zeehan
- The Eric Thomas Gallery Museum, Queenstown
- Mawson's Hut Replica Museum, Hobart
- Queen Victoria Museum and Art Gallery, Launceston
- Tasmanian Transport Museum, Hobart
- The Maritime Museum of Tasmania, Hobart

Your Own Family and Friends

Primary sources do not always have to be about famous people. Interviews with your family and friends are important too. Your grandmother might recall what your suburb used to be like. Friends can share stories about coming to live in Tasmania either from other states or from a country overseas.

Websites

Find more information about Tasmania on these websites:

- www.aboriginalheritage.tas.gov.au
- www.utas.edu.au/library/companion_to_tasmanian_history
- www.parliament.tas.gov.au

Glossary

bicameral - a government having two houses or sections
biosecurity - controlling plants, insects and animals that are harmful
circumnavigate - to sail all around a land mass
colonise - to settle in a new land and impose a new culture on the people living there
dialects - different forms of the one language
Elder - a respected Aboriginal person who is a custodian of traditional knowledge
half-mast - flying a flag halfway up the pole as a mark of respect when a community leader dies
infrastructure - buildings and physical services needed by a community
opiates - drugs derived from the opium poppy
plateau - a flat and high area of the landscape
pristine - clean and unspoiled
traditional ownership - the Aboriginal land ownership system in existence before the arrival of Europeans

Index

www.redbackpublishing.com.au